Life
and
a Glass of Milk

By

Vansh Sharma

First Published in Australia by Aurora House
www.aurorahouse.com.au

This edition published 2019
Copyright © Vansh Sharma 2019
Illustration: Swapna Sharma
Book interior and e-book design: Amit Dey
Cover design: Simon Critchell

The right of Vansh Sharma to be identified as Author of the Work has been asserted in accordance with the Copyright, Designs and Patents Act 1988.

ISBN number: 978-0-6485217-3-0 (Paperback)

A catalogue record for this book is available from the National Library of Australia

Distributed by:
Ingram Content:
https://www.ingramcontent.com/
    Australia: phone +613 9765 4800 |email lsiaustralia@ingramcontent.com
    Milton Keynes UK: phone +44 (0)845 121 4567 | email: enquiries@ingramcontent.com
    La Vergne, TN USA: phone 1-800-509-4156 | email: inquiry@lightningsource.com

Gardners UK:
https://www.gardners.com/
    phone +44 (0)1323 521555 | email: sales@gardners.com

Bertrams UK:
https://www.bertrams.com/BertWeb/index.jsp
    phone +44 (0)1603 648400 | email sales@bertrams.com

To my mum

ACKNOWLEDGMENTS

First and foremost, I am eternally grateful to my mum, Swapna, who gave me the power to believe in my passion and pursue my dreams. I couldn't have done this without her love and support. I love you, Mum! I am indebted to my dad, Vikas, for creating a loving family that has brought me immense motivation and inspiration to express my feelings into words.

I am deeply thankful to my grandma, Anjali, for feeding me delicious dishes, and to my grandpa, Vinod, for being a friend and a role model. I am truly grateful to my sixth-grade teacher, Mr McCool, for seeing the potential in me and encouraging me to continue writing poetry.

I would like to extend my sincere thanks to my uncle Anupam for helping me with the title of the book and to Aurora House Publishing, and especially to Linda and Sarah for believing in me – a twelve-year-old boy.

PREFACE

I wrote this book for the enterprise project – a major assignment that my teacher, Mr McCool, assigned in year six. When my classmates and I were deciding what we would do for our projects, I discovered that I'd done well at a poetry writing competition. This led to Mr McCool suggesting I write a book of poems for my assignment. I wasn't interested in the idea, as I wanted to do something cool: such as build a go-kart like some of my friends were doing. My mum and teacher's encouragement, though, persuaded me to start writing poems. My mum soon realised that I was able to write high-class poetry in a short amount of time. I didn't really believe her, and shrugged my shoulders. I continued to write more poems, though, inspired by the things around me, and soon was able to compose this very book.

CONTENTS

TRUTH

There are many reasons why
I would never lie
About my life
Even though it stabs me like a knife

You may sit and wonder
What good this may bring me
Whether this was a big blunder
Or my way of being free

This may seem quite too much
But for me it's never enough
You may ask why such
And I would respond without a bluff

You may ponder
My understanding is bizarre
But again the truth is that I do not want to squander
I want to live my life without a scar

My opinion is to always be honest
Even if it feels like the hardest thing to do
God brings no good to those dishonest
Being truthful is a gift which is true

People strive to be the best
This may be without honesty
This proves that they really aren't blessed
They realise they are living unwilling lives with dishonesty

Those menacing successful untruthful giants
Always get knocked down by their honesty backfiring
These are perfect examples of untruthful clients
In the future they find their life downwards spiralling

Honesty is the key to having a successful career
Without truth nothing can be done
You know dishonesty can stab back like a spear
You know it shoots back like a gun

I hope you read this over
To be fulfilled with realisation
If you do realise, you're as lucky as a four-leaf clover
If everyone is honest, they will create a strong nation

My guide is to follow the path of honesty and truth
To be friendly but righteous and good
Do this early when you are a youth
Will you do this? Yes, trust me, you would

Mark my word
This should be heard

Nothing Left

I've felt so empty since you've been gone
I haven't smiled at dusk nor dawn
I see no reason to feel elated
But I still try my best like you stated
Although sometimes I feel like ending it all to be up there with you
It would be incredible to be in a life so new
I know you won't be happy with this
So I try not to think about it and be full of bliss
I just want to see you or at least have a glance
That would be an awesome chance

THE BEACH

—❦—

I recall standing on a golden shore
With sea-spray washing over my face
And tasting the sharp taste
Of the salty wind brushing past
I see the waves reaching out to touch the shore
And feel the soft disappearing foam as they crash onto the sand
Clothing me with a thick layer of un-popped bubbles
I think of it as a place to think freely
With nothing around
Just the beach and me
Brightened by the unforgettable horizon
I crouch down and close my eyes
To ponder of what lies
Beyond that orange circle eating the ocean
If only I had a boat, I would sail to the end of the world
And then back again

If I had a Boat

—⚜—

If I had a boat, I would sail past the seven seas
Off to an unknown horizon
To watch the different people drifting by
To watch the ocean curl large waves unexpectedly
All I want is a boat
To breathe in the glamour of sailing
To feel the feeling of time rushing by
To be in a zone where no one can stop me
And in a place where time is not a thing
With my boat I would journey from country to country
Until I find the place perfect for me
Somewhere with the likes of me, a dreamland
If only I had a boat

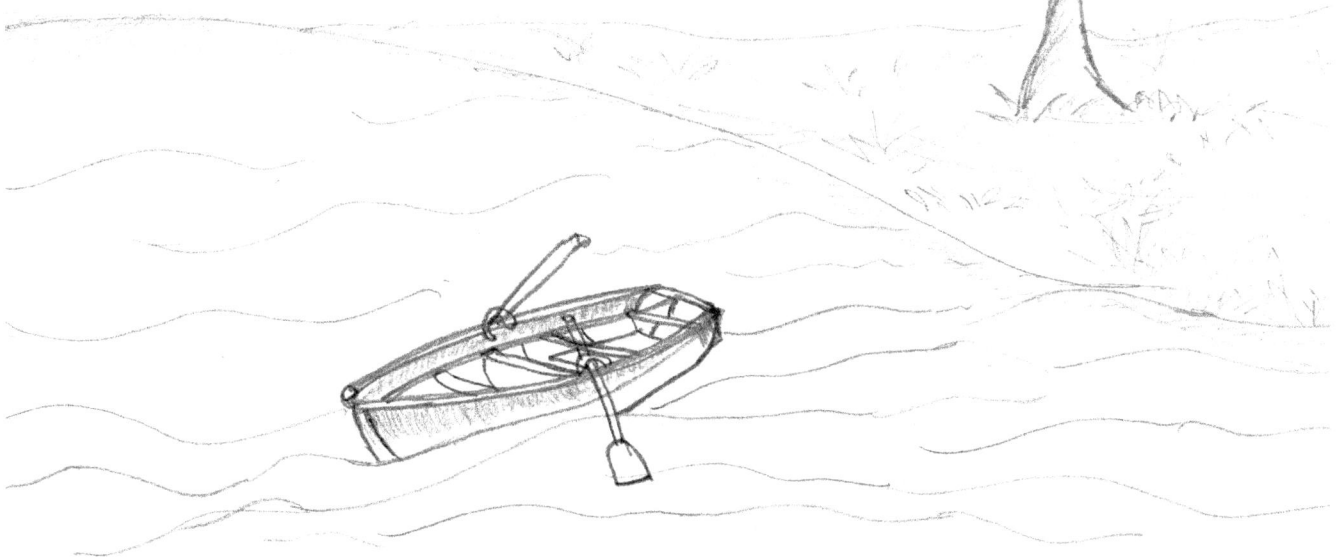

SUNRISE

—◦◦◦◦❦◦◦◦◦—

As the sun goes up its light slowly peers into my room
Indicating that today is a fresh new day
Watching the sunrise, I remind myself
To enjoy the present day, not the past – nor the future, as it is yet to come
The orange red sky clears my thoughts and fills it with the beauty of a new day
From the sun commencing to being high up
I stare at it through my bedroom window
Until it comes to an end

SUNSET

I arise from my bed
Woken up by orange glow of the sunrise
Soon to disappear
Behind a towering skyscraper
But I enjoy it while it lasts
As I watch the illuminated skyline
Of the buildings
It begins to peer lower to give way to the moon

SUNRISE TO SUNSET

sunrise
bright warm
glowing dawning arriving
after reaching the top of the world it descends
blazing flaming disappearing
radiant perfect
sunrise

THE HUMMINGBIRD

Over a rainbow
A hummingbird flies
Fluttering quietly
It sings a tune peacefully
While drifting to the other side

LIGHT TO DARK

—❧⸙❧—

light
bright glamorous
shining sparkling dazzling
the light gradually turns into dark
obliterating looming scaring
evilness deathliness
dark

Underwater

—◦◦⟡◦◦—

There's nothing like being underwater
Taking presence in the world below us
Amazed by fish in the cold water
Not having to be melancholy, no fuss
An eerie silence, with understanding
Thought being made through the prolonged quietude
Not a person to be heard commanding
Only fish to be seen nibbling at food
There's something mysterious about it
So undoubtedly extraordinary
I love it in a way, I will admit
Drifting through the water makes me merry
The underwater ... what a place to see
The underwater ... what a place to be

Harry's Torment – The Villanelle of the Rainbow

Harry couldn't stop thinking about the rainbow
It was just so bright and splendid
But he could never forget the show

That morning, Harry was shocked and said "whoa!"
He found himself feeling rather distended
And unable to stop thinking about the rainbow

Later, he realised that the rainbow was apropos
He thought the situation had become rather suspended
But he could never forget the show

Sarah said Harry was obsessing too though
Said his mind had become too unattended
But still Harry couldn't stop thinking about the rainbow

Harry took action like a row
The rainbow had sweetly ended
But he could never forget the show

Harry nosedived like a great big blow
His mind became dangerously offended
He couldn't stop thinking about the rainbow
But he could never forget the show

MY GOLD PUPPY

My gold puppy, you inspire me to write.
How I love the way you bark, eat and run,
Invading my mind all day and through the night,
I'm always dreaming about you, my kind son.

Let me compare you to a sanctuary…
You are more little, happy and gentle.
Snow chills the berries of January,
And wintertime has the clever fennel.

How do I love you? Let me count the ways.
I love your mental humour, smile and eyes.
Thinking of your flappy grin fills my days.
My love for you is the bold merchandise.

Now I must part away with a happy heart.
Remember my cold words whilst we're apart.

BIRDS IN THE PARK

An Azure Kingfisher
A Black-Necked Stork
A Blue-Winged Kookaburra
A Brolga
A Comb-Crested Jacana
An Egret
A Magpie Goose
A Partridge Pigeon
These birds flutter in the sunlight as I take a walk in the park
A Blue-Winged Kookaburra perches on a tree in the woodlands
While two Lorikeets and four Honeyeaters feast on the nectar
Of eucalyptus flowers
While Black Kites fly overhead.

THE BEAGLE

I fondly remember
I was once given a gift
In late December
The gift was pretty swift

The gift was a beagle
I asked my friend a question:
"Is the beagle legal?"
He was in deep depression

He said that we would die
As it was not permitted
Far, we would have to fly
Crime, we could have committed

We had flown to Britain
For I dearly loved beagle
Not once had he bitten
A beagle was not legal

To another nation
We were forced to travel to
Station after station
Beagle was hidden in a shoe

Far, far away we flew
To keep our poor, young beagle
We hoped he didn't get blue
A beagle just wasn't legal

We passed several miles
Just to save our cute beagle
We escaped court trials
As a beagle wasn't legal

We finally reached a country
Where a beagle was legal
Finally, we were free
For stuffed animal, Beagle

A Chocolatey Dream

My calm chocolate, you inspire me to write.
How I love the way you feed, look and eat,
Invading my mind day and night,
With me always dreaming about the warm treat.

Let me compare you to a light cherry.
You are more happy, amazing and bright.
Snow chills the berries of January,
And wintertime has the smart overnight.

How do I love you? Let me count the ways.
I love your personality and hands.
Thinking of your gorgeous smile fills my days.
My love for you is the quiet badlands.

Now I must hurry away with a blazing heart,
Remember my bright words whilst we're apart.

MY GOLDEN RETRIEVER

---※---

Why have you been away for so long?
You've made me cry and made me strong
I can't forget taking you for walks
Passing the tiny blocks
I remember you would stop and stare at the horizon closing in
I couldn't tell what your thoughts were and it would make my brain spin
I plead for you to tell me why, without notice, you left
After secretly making a small kitchen theft
You would depend on me and pull on my left shoelace
But now I feel better because I know you're in a better place

NEW YEAR'S DAY FIREWORKS

Fireworks, oh, fireworks, look at them burst
They definitely aren't the worst
Popping unexpectedly and dazzling in the night
Fireworks, oh, fireworks, shining, oh, so bright
From the fireworks, good vibes are being sent
Not a human to be seen suffering from lament
Crowds of people squeezed in like a tin of sardines
Fireworks, oh, fireworks, people are so keen
Bright colours to be seen all around
Not a fellow to be sighted on the ground
After the fireworks are finished, people are seen resting due to the long night
Then the sun soon rises and shines so bright to give everyone quite a fright
And later everyone is up to what feels like a new day
New Year's Day, oh, New Year's Day, a chance to say "yay!"

SIXTIETH BIRTHDAY!

—◦⟳◦✦◦⟳◦—

Oh, wow you have reached sixty!
You are much past the boring age of fifty
There is poise and elegance
In having so much experience
Even in Roman numerals you are now LX
Which means you truly are quite the best
So... excel yourself, and go
Into the next decade
Where Life may be even more eXcellent
May your spirit be free of crinkles
And, oh, those nasty little wrinkles
The angels are all smiling
Down from heaven today
For you were joyfully born
Sixty years ago on this very day
So, we would all like to wish you a very merry
Happy Birthday!

THE HOURGLASS

Sand passes through an hourglass quickly
But it takes time for the glass to be done
The sand passes through as though it's too thickly
To see that it's precise, I am stunned
When not looking, it feels as though it passes quite fast
And when staring desperately, slowly
It finishes, when the end sand grain falls last
Sooner or later, it's finished wholly
The sand goes through a small breach like a stream
The sand is used for ticking down the time
Like an ocean, the sand swims like a bream
The sand sparkles like a new silver dime
An hourglass, what a thing to be seen
An hourglass, what a thing to be clean

FIRE

---※---

F *Friendly firefighters incinerate.*
I *Intense wildfires quake.*
R *Reverberatory furnaces sinter.*
E *Eternal fires separate.*

THE CHASE

"Ahh!" the woman screamed
She was being chased by the dog
To be running from a dog, she had never dreamed
The dog kept bouncing onto the lady like a frog

The dog was determined to win
People would anger him and get under his skin
The woman did want to last
And, yes, she was pretty fast

She ran with the dog at her tail
And sprinted through the narrow trail
Then she entered the lift
Which was pretty swift

The dog would not give up this time
He had to be victorious
Young doggie knew that the woman was as sour as a lime
He would catch the woman who was so notorious

An Unusual Dream

We went on a walk
And had a little talk
We ventured through the forest
And killed the flowery florist
We chucked her in the river
And watched her go upriver
Her body soon floated through the bloody water
As we achieved the act of manslaughter
Then we kidnapped the granddaughter
Of little miss florist
Who had been walking through the forest
Finally the foul florist had been captured
We frolicked around enraptured
As her little good granddaughter had been saved
From being enslaved

THE TOOTH

Oh, what is worse than the great pain
Which drives me insane
It brings me a substantial shock
And makes anything edible taste like a rock
The coldness of an ice-cream
Challenges my boldness and makes me scream
How did this pain come over my tooth?
That's a hard question even for a sleuth
Oh, my terrible tooth

THE MUSTANG

—◦❦◦—

The engine roars as the Mustang starts up
The powerful exhaust blows leaves from its path
Ready to fire out for another drive
It can do great things with the engine of a V8
The eight massive pistons pump in and out
The car revs up loudly to be noticed once it's ready to race
The final tweaks are done
And the car stands, showing off its perfection
It slowly rolls onto the motorway
And vanishes into the distance

SUPERIORITY

—◦◦◦❦◦◦◦—

People always have some sort of superiority

But there is always a difference of how everyone uses it

Some citizens take the power and use it widely to become a better person

Although there are other people who use it without any caution

They regret their illiterate actions when they grow up to come to a realisation

As you can see there are two main types of people who use their power and superiority

Being unwise with mental strength can be a real issue in the long run

People should learn to capture righteous assets with their power that they hold as a person

The most successful people on this planet started out like each and every one of us

And in the beginning they didn't succeed at everything

But they were wise with their choices to become the best person they could be

They didn't speak to be where they are now

No, some couldn't even speak up or stand up for themselves

They accomplished their life's goal by taking action

So this is a message to everyone to excel themselves

And to use their power in a wise and respectful way

To become the person they want to be

A PAST

—◦◦◦❦◦◦◦—

I see a distant past left behind
Of someone ashamed to speak of their past
Something to be frightened of
Although failed with the real truth
Whether this may be disheartening or unspoken of
Something that reveals what really is the truth
This is the skin that no one hears about or sees
One can reveal the hidden
Or one can conceal what is already closed
That is the mysterious and irritating thought that lingers in one's mind
This can scar them for life
Or even worse, in circumstances,
If only one could be free from unwanted thoughts and desires

I WILL REMEMBER YOU

My heart beats a solemn tune
After you passed away so soon
I will remember you in heart and soul forevermore
For you are the one I will always adore
You vanished away from my life so fast
Oh, I wish it could last
You, I just want to embrace
But I know you are in a better place

DREAMING OF THE CIRCUS

Oh, how I wish I lived at the circus
With the clowns, acrobats, and animals
And let me tell you the purpose
Of not having friends as cannibals
Oh, how I wish I lived at the circus
Always performing night and day
The circus could never make me nervous
What a hard toil some might say
Oh, how I wish I lived at the circus

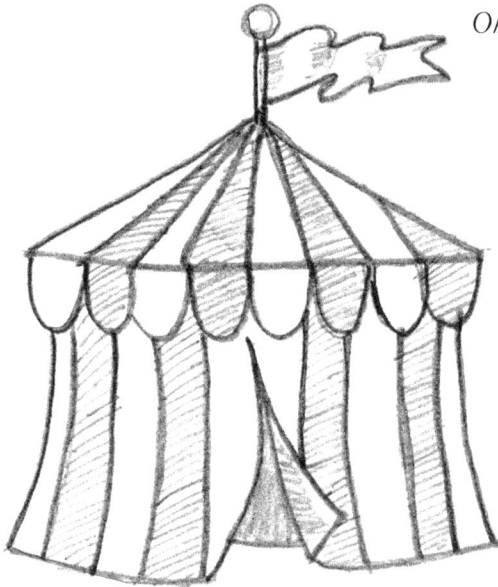

FLOATING ICE-CREAM

---◦◦◦✦◦◦◦---

Look at the ice-cream
Wafting elegantly through the sky
While singing a sweet lullaby
Oh, imagine how it would taste
Surely nothing like toothpaste
The satisfying crunch of the waffle cone
Definitely nicer than an old dog bone
A gentle lick of the soft ice-cream
Will send you into an everlasting dream
Ice-cream, oh, what a wonderful thing

YOU ARE THE FLOWER IN MY LIFE

What shall I compare to a flower?
What praises upon you shall now shower?
You are the best
For me, you yourself are a quest
A mystery waiting to be solved
That has me involved
You are the most unique
Please do kiss me on the cheek

FINGERPRINT

—◦◦◦◦✦◦◦◦◦—

The beauty of a fingerprint
Is seen in its details
The intricate curving lines producing something so unique
Curling into the centre
To look so pretty
One soul in the whole universe to be identified by this single fingerprint
Something so small yet so complex to be on the human body
What fascination this little masterpiece derives
Even though everyone holds it
But days pass without them recognising it
So meaningless yet so perplexed and sophisticated

LIFE

✦

There is no use of our lives
So do not tell me
These happy events that happen could belong with you or me
Should life have dealt a different hand
We need to view life for what it really is
Pointless, futile
And that it's hopeless, fruitless
There is no sense in it
Do not be so stupid to think that
The world can be looked at another way

LIFE

The world can be looked at another way
Do not be so stupid to think that
There is no sense in it
And that it's hopeless, fruitless
Pointless, futile
We need to view life for what it really is
Should life have dealt a different hand
These happy events that happen could belong with you or me
So do not tell me
There is no use of our lives

THE SKY

The sky above
Lies so blue
And appears to be clear from time to time
Sometimes crowded by flocks of birds
Sitting on the sunburnt sand
And watching the waves break down is heart-warming
The seagulls call in the distance
Behind me is a horrible array of flashing lights
With the irritating noises of cars
But I am able to ignore
The busy city and focus on what nature has to bring

SUMMER

Summer arrives with a wave of heat
Which overwhelms its victims
Increasing the temperatures greatly
Summer's like the devil of the seasons with its heat
People walk onto the beach
Only to find the soft sunburnt sand
They dip into the sea of cool water
And take a break from what summer has to bring

AUTUMN

The breeze whooshes past, scattering leaves throughout the street
Telling people that Autumn has finally arrived
Little do they know that the robber has already stolen their emeralds off their trees
And has replaced them with brown, red, and orange colours
Later, residents notice the colours of the leaves changing
They stand and stare at them in their humble vicinity
They keep watch of the red and orange colours that build up the patrol of trees
Autumn stays for a few months while stealing more wanted emeralds
It then leaves with its pot of gold with a smile on its face
Hoping to come back next year
Nobody knows what happens to the emeralds stolen by Autumn
But we do know that more shining green leaves grow back
Later to be reclaimed by Autumn's greed
But not to forget its worthy apprentice… the wind
The wind is a vital part in helping its boss, Autumn
It creates a distraction for the passers-by
So that Autumn can go easily about its business
After another year of hard work, the boss and its apprentice share their earnings
And look forward to next year

WINTER

—◦◦◦◦❦◦◦◦◦—

Winter stays sly
And loathsome of spring
As it ruins the splendid work
Of the bare trees
To grow back the leaves it deserves
Winter works away secretly
Covering the lands with sheets
Over sheets of snow
Then it rests after accomplishing its duties

SPRING

—◦⋅❦⋅◦—

Spring arrives with a bang
As it blooms the leaves once again
With its vibrant colours
It defeats the harmful wrath of Winter
And leaves the many lands
With its gifts of freshness and colours
After Spring completes its duties
It watches over its wonderful creation
And the blessed people living in it

Season's Blessing

How greatly blessed are the people on earth
To have four outstanding seasons
Of cold and warmth
Of seasons with piles of snow such as Winter
And Autumn with great amounts of foliage
Summer full of heat
And Spring the regrowth of new fresh leaves
What an amazing world we live in

RAIN

The rain pitter-patters upon the earth
And leaves a pleasing smell of petrichor
It drenches everything with its fresh water
And fills the drought-stricken lakes
It provides us with its water so pure
So that we can drink nature's pleasing liquid
On the window I can see
The little round balls of water plummeting down upon the glass
What a beautiful sight
With its repeating tune, silence is created in its surroundings
What a pretty thing is rain

COCKATOO

"Cockatoo,"
I said walking by the road
Watching
The white-feathered parrot
I felt the peace that radiated
From its vibrant white feathers
And its determined black dots for eyes
I giggled at the yellow hairs that protruded
From the top of its head
Seeing it for the first time.
Without known reason
My heart felt contented
Maybe it was because of the longing I had
To just catch a glimpse
Of this sign of what I thought was peace
I continued my journey
Smiling

Hop Goes the Rabbit

Among the bushes
A small bunny rabbit hops
Bouncing joyfully
With its feet it beats a tune
While returning to its humble abode

WHAT'S AROUND US

⸺◦⸱◦⸱◦⸺

Thy beauty shall always be admired
Of the nature surrounding us today
Everything around us should be desired
Everything has something to portray

VIVID LIGHTS

—◦◦◦◦◦◦◦✦◦◦◦◦◦◦—

Vivid lights is what one sees
While travelling through a nature-like city
On one's journey he sees a hive of bees
Gathering together like a small committee

A Frightening Dream

—◦∞◦❦◦∞◦—

I sat curiously, waiting quietly,
White mist wafted by, approaching me often
It thrashed around violently
Like a fatal zombie raised from its coffin

THE WOMAN AND HER SON

He came crying home
And wept
In his mother's lap
He cried,
"Throw your arms around me."

PARROTS

The old noisy parrots
mimic the sound of near creatures—
repeating

The Butterfly

A butterfly flutters quietly
Soaring high in the sky—
It stops on a flower

THE NIGHTINGALE

—◦◦◦✦◦◦◦—

A bird sings a meaningful song
Heard in all directions
Repeating

SEAGULL

---

flapping its wings
the seagull soars
to the everlasting horizon

A WHALE CALLS

---ᘒᘓᘖ⊹ᘗᘔᘑ---

A whale's call is heard in water
It echoes
Decreasing gradually

Autumn Thief

———◦◦◦✦◦◦◦———

Autumn arrives like a thief
stealing the delicate leaves—
disappearing

WRONG-DOING

—◦◦◦✦◦◦◦—

We're all hurt by consequences
Caused by our fiendish acts
Backfiring

EFFECT

The stillness of water is disrupted
by a single drop
rippling

DEATH

———⟡———

It comes when least wanted
It goes never
Without knowing it comes—
death

THE SNOWFLAKE

It floated down
Onto his cheek
And seemed to gently caress him
Only momentarily
Before gliding onto his shoulder,
Staying there for a few seconds
To soon join its white family
In the snow

LIFE POETRY

—⟨∙⟩—

Soft, comfy single bed waiting to be used again
Wooden study table holding up heavy files
Several mountains of books stacked into enormous towers
Wooden drawers filled with little bits and pieces
A large white wooden cupboard concealing escaping clothes
Massive shelves stuffed with old dusty books

Light orange paint surrounding the house like a warm embrace from Gran
Backyard accurately cut by the experienced and invaluable hands of Grandpa
Wired backyard fence coated with bushy emerald shrubs guarding the garden
Rolling around on the bright front lawn beside the purple leaves brushing past my ankles
Small narrow dark alleyway leading out towards the greenery
Crystal clear pool reflecting against the verandah wall, covering it with tiny waves

The tranquillity around the smooth Parramatta River is sensational
The calm and friendly people always wanting to help you out in your duties
The tall Meriton building towering over the city of Parramatta, standing proudly like an army general on parade
The several wineries breeding rich wine because of the many vineyards
The busy citizens of Sydney city bustling hurriedly to their work places
Harbour Bridge protecting Darling Harbour and its large body of water

Uluru, the heart of the country, holding us together like a family
Recalling the Australian and New Zealand Army Corps (ANZAC) who fought to save our nation in the Great War
All the natural disasters controlled by strong forces formed of people ensuring we are not taken away
Parliament House keeping in all the important people ruling our nation righteously
All the warm beaches covered with proud Aussies relaxing after their hard labour
Beautiful landscapes of greenery and desert-cherishing wonderful memories

Ancestors who fought in the many rough and gruesome wars, making it through, that is the reason I am alive today
Born in the vast fields of Manchester filled with everlasting sunshine and friendly people
The streets of India smelling of strong and rich spices being sold at stalls
All warm and cosy inside the small flat in Scotland, keeping out the freezing breeze and frost

Saving citizens from harmful problems, aiding them and allowing them to continue enjoying their awesome life
Waking up to hear the laughter and excitement of my kids on weekends, wanting to have a lot of fun, awaiting wonderful experiences
Staring out of the window, knowing that I have achieved my life's goal

ABOUT THE AUTHOR

*V*ansh Sharma is 12 years old and is currently studying in year 7 at Sydney Grammar. He enjoys writing poems and strives to write many more to add to his anthology. He aspires to become an established poet one day. Everyday objects, feelings, and phenomena are constantly inspiring his poetry.

www.ingramcontent.com/pod-product-compliance
Lightning Source LLC
Chambersburg PA
CBHW061407090426
42739CB00022B/3498